THE GIRL FROM ERMITA

THE GIRL FROM ERMITA

& selected poems

1961–1998

Goh Poh Seng

*For Colin Barron
with thanks for your helpful
friendship.
Best,
Poh Seng
May 10ᵗʰ 2002.*

NIGHTWOOD EDITIONS

Published by
NIGHTWOOD EDITIONS
R.R.#5, S.26, C.13
Gibsons, BC Canada V0N 1V0

Cover design by Kajin Goh / King Hajo Graphik
Author photograph by Jack Bastow
Printed and bound in Canada

Nightwood Editions acknowledges the financial support of
the Government of Canada through the Book Publishing
Industry Development Program and the Province of British
Columbia through the British Columbia Arts Council, for its
publishing activities.

Canadian Cataloguing in Publication Data

Goh, Poh Seng, 1936–
   The girl from Ermita and selected poems 1961–1998

   ISBN 0-88971-167-4

   I. Title.
PS8563.0822G57 1998   C811'.54   C98-911054-0
PR9199.3.G596G57 1998

THE CANADA COUNCIL | LE CONSEIL DES ARTS
FOR THE ARTS | DU CANADA
SINCE 1957 | DEPUIS 1957

For Margaret

My beloved

CONTENTS

SPRING MOON BLUES

from EYEWITNESS

M E M O R Y

Afterwards there's nothing left,
save memories hovering like
gulls round a departing ship,

which draws away gathering
conciseness of a shape
till it comes to terms with the sea.

It now belongs to me,
the sea in its entirety,
but am I increased?

SINGAPORE

Day here hurls its light

And there is scant comfort
to be had
in this form of conclusion

There are always those wakeful
watching
for a consolation

Thoughts drift by
wash of some season
the ships put out to sea

The tide by Katong side recedes
retracts a promise
only tentatively given

Towards the sea's fresh salt
the river bears pollution
whose source was simple hills

Whose migration was tainted
when man
decided to dip his hand

Nourishing his wants
a commercial waterway
greased with waste

Barges bearing rubber
rattan, white copra
to other appetites

Waiting sedate in harbour
the ocean berths vessels
like cars in a car park

Heeding the *mandore*'s bark
puny bent backs
turn to ceaseless toil

In this betrayal of soil
pliant refuse
the sun rears heaps

In *godowns* by the wharfs
such heaps are seen
piled high by a dream

But in due decline
the sun dips
and shadows become larger hills

By night ships outside
lie disparate
like separate destinies

Landward fear lurks
in neonlit streets
entices thugs to seize

Night here grows its dark.

UNKNOWN DREAMS

I lie a part of the tall grass
that has a smell of wet and green
facing the wind-made
tremulous leaves above
and as they tremble
they make a sound
and turn patches of sky into light.

I suck in the earth's might
feeling it strong on my back
while the sky becomes a bottomless well
into which I might drop the next second.
I feel easily dislodgeable
like a parachutist falling,
falling into sleep
to stir a heap of unknown dreams.

THE HAVENOTS

Our night is small with whispers
of people cowered by their voices,
our poor repertoire of lamps
only probes the darkness,
feeble torches
flickering upon ribbons of wind,
until the red idea of dawn dares again
and our gathering cries rise in clamour.

We have only our clamour
we brandish high, a flag,
high in the strong winds,
but however high the winds waft, it must fall.

So what is the point of standing around
nursing the pale moon in our palm?

DROUGHT

For weeks now the burgeoning sun
spreads into a static whiteness;
a protracted noon during which
nothing stirs.
Our several sharp-edged shadows
and those of trees and stones
lie spread-eagled on the hard ground:
so many broken Icaruses.

The leaf-less trees cringe inert,
skeletal under the mocking sky,
while vultures prowl sullen, only
a momentary darkening.
Cracks index the parched earth,
caked firm, inhospitable to seed.
We rave and dream of cool rain,
rain, a piston, a pulsing in our blood.

But nothing comes.
We are a patient people,
our patience fashioned by long history.
And buried beneath the silt of centuries,
our soil a compost of our fathers
grudged us, even in good days
a sparse harvest.
Even in good days.

Now drought ages our soil an enduring brown,
the colour of despair
but still victim to the sun's songs.
Yet if the drought persists,
everything will ignite and become
fuel, to black fumes
16   rising fiercely like fame to the sky.

VIETNAM 1967

Beginning another vigil
he regards the tentative sun
through a fragmented sky;
otherwise there is only greenness.
In the still quiet dawn
he downs a mug of tea,
leans his rifle against a tree
and now and then recalls his home
unearths another day.
He is far from his hamlet.

It was an unquestioning life,
tilling the stubborn land that defies
the controlling hand of man.
There was consolation, now he knows
the laughter of his child,
the softness of his wife
who yielded to him at night.
So what if kingdoms topple?

His dream shakes the silent air.

He sees his home gutted in the sun,
he sees his wife, head blown off,
the body of his child strewn
among young stubble of padi.

For days he prowled that waste
unable to quell his hate.
How to mobilize that precise pain?

Time passes.
Now and then a recall of home:
she chants at night to their child
who smiles, remembering small mischiefs.
After losing them,
their absence remains.

He makes his fists into a power
fierce as one whose sinews
could manage the sun.

In the glare of the sun
the planes beautiful
like silver spears
come in an eddy of air.

Amongst battered tree trunks
his blood splatters
into uncanny flowers.

Over the gentle contour of hills
and the sea,
the happy young crew from afar
returns to the air.

THE GNOME'S GROWTH

Born after the primeval dawn
With opaque eyes facing the void,
He grew up through a thick fabric
Of congenital lies and Pavlovian faiths,
Assisted by a gangrenous hate
That now and then emerged gingerly:
A sapling through tight soil,
Desire through tight lips.

Somewhere green was a youth,
A cosy past, congealed in tableaux,
Which, he knew, were mere facades:
Absurdity was always lurking
There behind the masks.

Possessed with a burning itch for normalcy,
He grew up bent,
Spending time in pubescent scratchings,
Spawning shoals of throbbing lives:
Singly confined in completeness,
Singly completely dies.

He prowled the febrile yellow wastes
Fuming fiercely like a caged beast,
Always encountering day,
The sucking heat sucking away
His hissing strength.

Guarding his sanity with a
Constant meticulous cautiousness,
Until it finally cracked,
And leaking into his head was
A dark, heavy cloud that
Dragged and enmeshed.

O block out the sun!
Dampen down its rays which
Agitate his restless soul,

And let him be, let him lie,
Soothingly tending to himself:
For even in hell,
One can attend to oneself.

DREAMLAND

I have burst through a moment out of time
becoming memberless and afloat in a between.
I am no longer the minstrel, historic time,
walking in the dereliction of man's land
amongst heaps of dead and doomed dreams
and amongst the boom, the cacophony
of carefully motivated actions.

I have arrived in the solvent dreamland of inaction.

THE OLD FISHERMAN
OF SONGKLA

To this open bay, a blue water
gritted by taciturn brown rocks,
the repetitive waves file
slips and slivers of white.

The old fisherman,
face inscribed with age,
net held painstakingly in hand,
scours for tell-tale signs of fish,
eyes earnest, sharp as fish hooks.

Then throws the chain-weighted net
casting a delicate skein,
hauls a few silvery-scaled,
mouth-gasping fish
onto the hot, grating sand.

When he makes his meal at night,
a memory is brought back of the sea,
and he dreams, perhaps of his drowning.

SUNBATHING

You know nothing of the city,
our city does not permit
even a memory of the sky.

My daily life
make up my days
the same without let up.

O for a windfall of days
that are without deliberation,
without architecture.

The sun a burgeoning eye
at point blank
on me.

Let my long-untaught senses
simmer then,
excite a blunt consciousness.

SNAPSHOT

The woman drags a dog on a leash,
herself pushing hard against a forward wind;
a man studies them at ease from behind,
I smile secretly at our secret wishes.

TEA PARTY

It maybe peaceful, amenable
to cease being concerned
and slide into a comfortable existence,
incline myself to indulgences
out of a hee-hee life,
a do-ray-me dimension,
a snug little life –
and then be suitably reconciled
to having jam with toast, with tea,
under some shade-spreading tree
with any old he or she
or just me, with my money.

ON LOOKING AT THE MOON AND THINKING

I realize I cannot expect my life
to change overnight
or over many nights
or, for that matter,
over many years.
So you can say
if you want to,
that I have really
not been hopeful,
hoping.

But then, what can I do, but do?

THE CRIPPLE

It's futile to believe
that sky will not fatigue
like flesh
sags with wrinkles,

See how it flops with age
on the ledge of night,
decomposing,
garish with colours,

Blackness quickens
beneath the trees.
My shadow lengthens,
thin and light-footed,

A would-be Quixote
ready to wander away
in quest of dreams
or of anything.

But me, I remain
feet firm on the ground,
crippled
by the immensity of choices.

EXILE IN A COLD LAND

In a winter air when bare trees
inlay calligraphics in the sky,
snow flutters perhaps
from a grey distance,
and trailed by his own voice,
a lone man walks,
afraid of being smothered,
immured in a white universe.

Night by night he threatens
to jettison the stars,
evict them in tumbles
as snow from a frozen sky,
else dreams the thin-sheeted ice
cracks beneath his feet,
fragile as a brief handshake.

MINDSCAPE

I

Web-clasped to dead beams
In an unlit littered corner where
Time stops assuming its movement
And drips dry: stiffened to a speck,
The flesh of fruit has rotted away.
It leaves a black pip that had hid
Stubborn in its pith,
Since its being was named,
And though unknown, unheeded,
A heart it was: geiger-ticking.

Stratum upon stratum of days weigh
And by virtue of weight,
Fall compact into unhurrying
Like an air-leaking,
Collapsing concertina.

II

Soot in the cities darkens the air
Where spirit seeks to persecute,
To sack the lair of crowds,
But sleek like sleeping seals
In some noon pavilion of the sea,
They notice not the stare,
The eager interception crouching
Alert in their fecund forest.

But spirit, like the wind,
Tapers out, worn by distance,
And the wanderer, suspirance seeking,
Waits for what seems not to come,
Not to come his way.

III

So clasp a mask onto the face,
Walk all similar,
Not dissimilar to black taxis

In the rain.
For much effort has been spent
In antagonizing the throng,
Only ending up winning the intimacy
Of the ones that were scorned.

Either share in this communal warmth,
Else slide into the breathing
Shadow of corporeal love
To exult an unscrupulous
Passion in the dark.
Thus drowsed by this ancient
Lineage of expediencies
That heaps onto one, asleep,
An edifice of familiar leaves.

IV
Until the last hope is lost,
When clouds at their outposts
All come out of abeyance
To close dark upon my world.
Until the seas, bereft of motion,
Heave and spray no more,
Calling for a visitation
To her cavernous pregnancy,
Her spaciousness of
Aquamarine and greens,
Where all senses sink,
Disintegrate by diffusion.

Then only shall I fall
Intense, reverent before
A tabernacle of stillness and darkness
Where automatic fingers play
Upon the beads of immutability.
The spirit of this solitary seeker
Disembodied forever by finality,
Or near finality.

V

In some seasonless zone of sea
Which has profound intentions
That know not perfect clarity,
Where mute fish and rhythmic anemone,
Cliffs of corals and solemn crabs
All become as mirages,
A hand reaches out
Meaning to placate,
Yet withholding something
Between touches to
Awake a terrible craving.

The divulgence of seminal dreams
Initiates the currents, churns up
The seas into advancing cavalcades of
Waves upon waves of spumes,
Unleashing onto the beach,
Like phlegm of sickly fishes,
A castaway, whose identity was
Finally unconcealed:
Me! Me! Me!

DUBLIN NEWSBOY
IN THE SNOW

Huddling in the contracting cage
    of that outside air,
dodging the shooting trajectories
    of cosy cars,
    a lean boy,
weaned from unattainable hopes
    and distant glitters,
dips within himself to God
    but hears no reply.
Instead, only
    the passive descent of snow
covers his face with placid kisses.
    He crouches
with his sodden ware,
    crushing some snow into balls,
wishing, wishing,
    but not daring
to hurl them at the passersby,
    whirling like the snow
by his passing world.

SOME WORDS
written in Manila and La Union Province,
Philippines, while attending the Afro-Asian
Writer's Symposium, in February, 1975 (for
Chielo R. Banal)

4 a.m.
Silence now.
Silence at last.
Most of Pasay City asleep,
    Quezon and Manila too.
4 a.m.
        the proper thing to do.
            It's very human,
though the curfew lifts
        that invisible veil
we're unaware of it,
            everywhere and always
unaware, unaware.

So there's silence outside.
    Yes, silence,
but within my skull
    stalk
        your words, my words,
            our words,
        words, words
    rattling within
like stones in an egg shell.

        Words can kill.
Don't we know yet
        words, words
are both communion and ammunition?
        I'm tired.
    It's merely human.

My bones limpid with fear
    and contempt for words.
    My blood made lava

circulating and circulating
　　an unwanted stream
and yet, and yet
　　　when it ceases:
　　　　I die.

　　　We're a people
who love too much,
　　　said Nita,
　　　　　who did.
　　　And a people
who talk too much,
　　　said Jose,
　　　　　who did.
　　　And a people
who trust too much,
　　　said Juan,
　　　　　who did.

But why me?
　　　A poet only.
　　　an artificer of words,
　　　a fool,
　　　a lurer,
　　　a lover,
　　　a conjurer,
　　　a coward,
　　　a knave,
　　　a compulsive listener
　　　and talker,
　　　a man only,
　　　who
　　　long ago
　　　should have had his
　　　　　tongue
　　　coated with confetti and shit
　　　　　surely
　　　plucked out!

His ears
stoppered!

Ah Juan,
don't you know
   you must
   your trust
  weighs my soul?
And
   Jose,
don't you know
   you must
   your openness
  stirs my anger?
And
   Nita,
      especially Nita,
don't you know
   you must
   your love
  only sheds your blood?

So, this junket,
for that was what I thought
      it was
      before coming
      to Manila,
         to
   this solemn symposium
   of Afro-Asian writers
      has turned out
         differently:
   not a junket
because, Juan
   you offered more
      than hospitality,
and Jose,
   you gave your most

                precious possession
                        your life in my hands,
and Nita,
Oh Nita,
        who lavished your love on me –
                finding myself
                        I return.

You are all killing me,
                friend now,
                and brother now,
                        and lover now.

And I shall depart no longer
                an official guest,
but as friend, and brother and lover

leaving in my wake
                our words
which are killing you,
                killing you,
        I know, I know
                and you, me,
                and me, you,
                and you, me,
                        together,
                        TOGETHER.

SPRING AT WU LING

after Li Ch'ing Chao

A smell of rotting flowers
as the wind settles here

Each evening I grow weary
of having to comb my hair

My man is gone. How tedious
now the same old affairs

So let these tears suffice
there is little to add

The spring is still fine
they say, at Wu Ling

I could set myself adrift
on a light grass-hopper boat

But it would likely find
this melancholy too much a load.

THINKING OF
THE POET TU FU

Strolling out into the evening after work
before the dew settles on the grass,
the sky without a cloud is as wide
and is the colour of the sea;
so much so, the little dark boats in the distance
seem to be moving up to it;
I think of you, old grey-haired Tu Fu,
how this kind of setting
and this time of day
would move you to sing one of your poems.

Towards the west the same sun is setting
making dark the trees in my garden,
throwing large shadows on the grass
while Kasan, my young son
runs about, noisily playing
soldiers with his friend.
I wonder whether you approve
who have written so much against wars?

Alas, my friend, we too have our
endless wars, one thousand
two hundred and fifty odd years
after you have lamented,
"Wars still not ended" . . .
in Vietnam
the Middle East
now Czechoslovakia
and Biafra!
When Kasan is older, I shall tell him.

Now my good wife is cooking
our evening meal in the kitchen;
I wish we could have you to dinner
and though I have no jugs of millet wine,
I'll get a few beers from the 'fridge.
How we would talk and talk,
my friend.

In the fading light
little swallows are having their last fly;
a lone sea hawk surveys overhead
then dives for its prey . . .
my place at Lim Chu Kang
overlooks the Johore Straits.
The small *sampans* are returning,
each boat has a tiny, uncertain lamp.
Already the distant hills
are melting into the night.

Once the sun has dipped
it is so far away,
farther than the stars.
Our life has become a small matter
though our anxieties loom large.
Thinking of you,
it is so easy
to span the years.
These twelve centuries or more
have really wrought little change;
the condition of man remains
much the same, much the same.

My wife calls;
dinner is ready.
Dear girl, she has read
all my poetry and asked
when I would write
one for her.
She should know
she matters more to me
than all my poetry.
I think you would
understand that,
my old grey-haired Tu Fu.

from LINES FROM BATU FERRINGHI

LINES FROM BATU FERRINGHI
SATURDAY, 20TH JULY, 1974

Green upon green
The hills roll
Beyond green,
Undulant,
Are lit
By fresh
Sunlight.

And I
Enter
Into this morning.

Regarding
This assortment of hills
Arraigned behind the road,
Their outlines sweeping,
Smooth, compliant,
Their hard structures, bones,
Hidden by the clotted green
Strewn thick as plush down.

Thinking,
Am in need of hills,
Am in need of
The simplicity,
The meanings deepening
Out of reach
Of the mind.

Things
That the mind
Knows not of!
Always!

That we are ignorant
And the mind relinquishes
Lets loose

To rove
In rarer air,
Brings solace,
Is that much
Minus the pressures,
And in reticence
Rises with time
Up into the light,
Attains comeliness
In the far recesses
Of the hills.

And to lose
All there is
All we want
All our wants

Is a task
Exceeding
Most strengths;
Is a task
We're not equal to.
Always!

We seem so incapable
Of learning,
Never seizing
The chance to change.

What I do,
Having survived the night,
Is to shed my night-self,
A piece of self
Let fall
Like a petal
Whose freshness is lost,
Discarded
By the wayside.

Now,
In broad daylight,
Improvise a new expediency—
The night and its history,
Obliterated.

For there lurk
Promises of fresh pleasures
Where the earth trembles
Under a hot sky,
The minute shadows
Abiding beneath the trees
In the hills
Frolic,
Under wood
Shapes of light and shade
Shift in motion,
Like the bottom of the ocean.

I head
Where the green hills are,
To locate nymphs
Sporting in a sylvan arena
So that I may
Impound their jubilance.
I follow a tiny, unpaved
Path that led
Through a small *kampung*,
Passing children at play,
Hens picking at the dirt
And a black duck,
While birds chirped
Ceaselessly above.
At length,
I stumble onto
A Malay restaurant
called Din Bamboo.

Within, I was welcomed
By an old Malay man
With a thin, kind face
And warm, friendly eyes
Who introduced himself
As "Din Bamboo",
Or "Pak Din".
"Everyone calls me Pak,
Or father," he said.
His real name's Din Bin Tahib.

He sat at the simple wooden table
And chatted with me
In Malay
While I sipped hot, black coffee.

He has made friends
With people
From fifty-four countries!
They've all come
To his unpretentious restaurant
A little off the beaten track,
Tucked away in this *kampung*.
Pak Din showed me stacks
Of photo albums,
Piles of postcards and letters,
And several notebooks –
Assorted memorabilia
Of his friends
From fifty-four countries.

Fingering through them
Is like encroaching upon
A host of ghosts,
Is like catching them
Unawares
Daydreaming,
Beyond the reach of time.

All those faded photographs,
Sepia-tinted,
Of faces attacked by time,
And so pale
They slip away
Float in the air
Choosing the ambience of leaves
Which ripple in the breeze.
Within the crumbling pages
Of the books and albums,
Their cheeks are no longer warm
Upon which a lover might press,
And no hot breath
Issues from the drained petals
Of their lips,
The light in their eyes
Gutted out,
No longer questioning
The empty air;
They simply stare
Without surprise,
Without the sparkle of passion.
Embalmed,
Stranded out of time,
They are not
At home there.

No one was about
That late morning,
Only a few scrawny chickens
Scratching the dry earth
Out in the drab frontyard.

"Business is bad lately,"
Pak Din said sadly,
"But there were good times!"
– Remembering his visitors
From fifty-four countries.

"There was a time
When I used to gross
$100 to $200 a day!
Until March this year
When the police cracked down
On the hippies,
The young foreigners,
Believing all of them
To be drug addicts.
Nowadays, I hardly collect
$20 to $30 a day.
So life has become hard.
I've eight children of my own
You know," he declared,
Half-boastfully,
Eyes twinkling with mischief –
A little proud he was, a man,
And also a little worried.
"Most of my children are young,
Still schooling.
Allah! How to feed them all?
How to look after them?"

He paused a moment or two,
Looking up at the hot zinc roof
Above us
And beyond it –
But the solution
Was not up there.
Never has been.
He rolled a reed cigarette,
Lit it: when his eyes
Returned to me,
He was smiling.
"My *rokok ekonomi*,"
He joked, indicating
His cheap, reed cigarette.

"Not *rokok istimewa*,
Or society cigarette,
As the ads went.
The old man
Enjoyed a simple laugh.

"Would you like lunch?"
He asked.
"All right, Pak!"

"There's only fixed lunch.
I hope you don't mind.
Very simple,
Very cheap.
Only $1.50."

"That's fine."

He went into the kitchen,
A dingy, side room
Behind the counter
Arrayed with soft drink bottles
To prepare my lunch.

Later, as I ate
My plate of plain rice
And the small dishes
Of fish curry, an egg omelet,
A bowl of boiled white cabbage
And a circular disc of pineapple
In a peanut and chilli sauce,
Pak Din related his story,
Constantly pulling
On the thin reed cigarette
As if it might assist him
To draw a firm conclusion
From his own tale.

He had been brought up in Kedah,
His family of Trengganu stock.
Back in Kedah
He'd been a *bomoh*
And a *bersilat* master.
Later on, he took to sea,
Became a fisherman
Here in Penang.
But life was hard.
It was difficult
To make a living from the sea.
Though he had fought
His share of black storms,
Had braved the untamed waves,
He could not earn enough
To support his family.
So he took a job
As a worker
On a fish trawler.

Pak Din said he saw
With his own eyes
How the trawler fleets
With their equipment, their nets,
Took everything from the sea,
Even scraping the bottom,
Churning up the spawning beds,
The rich breeding sanctuaries,
He's not surprised
There are few fish now
For the poor inshore fishermen
Working their small *sampans*.

I asked whether
Many of the *kampung* folk
Were fishermen.
Pak Din gestured
With an empty wave

Of his brown, bony hand.
"Most of them
Have given up the tradition –
They're no longer
Men of the sea.
They go to work for a wage
At the hotels by the beach,
Or at the factories
In Butterworth."

When my meal was eaten,
I continued to sit there
Through the hot afternoon,
Sipping black coffee,
And sharing cigarettes with the old man.
Sometimes, he would lapse into silence,
Staring absently beyond the room,
Beyond the village,
As if far, far out to sea.
Sometimes, he would talk excitedly
About his past experiences.

He related some of his amazing cures
As a *bomoh*.
There was a rich, Chinese *towkay*
Whose body was already dead
When Pak Din was called
To attend to him;
His body had turned
White and cold –
Only his mouth was moving
Though he could not make a sound.
Pak Din took herbs and native medicine,
Covered the man's body with them
And then bound him up.
He thought the sick man
Had to stay wrapped up
For at least five days,

So serious was his condition.
But after three days,
The sick man began to stir!
He struggled weakly
With his arms and feet –
He, who was already dead
Except for his mouth!
One and a half days later,
The patient couldn't stand it anymore
And struggled violently loose
From his swaddling of herbs and medicines.
When he was unwrapped,
A terrific stench was given off –
It was the mixture of medicines
And his long sickness,
Pak Din said.
The man recovered fully,
Is still alive
And grateful to this day –
All that happened
Back in Kedah.

Although he has tried
To stop practising as a *bomoh*,
People still come to him
Because of his reputation.
He spoke of how he'd cured
A young American
Who was suffering
From drug withdrawal.
Pak Din, gesticulating
In his cane chair,
Enacted how
He'd placed his right hand
Over the boy's face
And pulled away his sickness
With his powers.
A few years later,

The young man
And his parents
Came back to Penang
To thank Pak Din.
They even presented him
The T shirt he was wearing –
With wide blue and white stripes
Like a football jersey.
They also gave him
A Japanese transistor set.

The soft drone of life
In the *kampung*
Incubates in the afternoon.
Suddenly, I recognized
The months of similar,
Empty afternoons ahead
For this kind, old man;
And I feared, I hope falsely,
That days would cave in
Under his frail weight.

"You know, people
Have visited me here
From fifty-four countries!"
Pak Din repeated.
"The world has been to my place.
Anytime I want to,
I can visit my children
From these faraway countries
And they will hug me,
Call me Pak, father,
Out of love,
For I love them all!
I would really like
To visit America and Australia
Where I have so many friends,
Before I die."

Soon, I took leave of Pak Din,
Outside, the light was so bright
It blurred my sight.

As I walked away,
I wondered whether,
        Years later,
I would still remember,
        This day,
And this man,
        Who is not a myth,
But real.

from **BIRD WITH ONE WING**

P R O L O G U E

Follow the bird that flies into the dream,
don't hold back from uncharted greens
misused from a first, miraculous dawn
when all was implicit, never neutral:
each moment an unrenewable crystal.

Only the sane few'd likely harvest rainbow beams
woven out of white light, whose seam-
less threads dance in being when born;
the heart laid bare bears inadmissible
flowers, promises colours to others irreconcilable

As fugitives seeking forever that brutal harmony, wing-
ing with the same swift bird into the dim
interior, through the wild woods storm;
engendered in blood, the poem rises, simple,
its roots forgotten, its force strategic, incomprehensible.

Pulau Hujong
April, 1982

FROM EARTH

In a fallow age,
    O I want
to sow my eyes
      on an orange wind,
plow my flesh
      in a blue dawn,
    so that
my bones might ripen
      in the sun;
      and when
the marrow bursts,
      unbridled,
it will spill forth grain
      rushing into gold,
gilded by the heat
      and by the seasons,
    so that
        in good time
there will be
    seas of it
      and seas of it
    rippling
      upon a green breeze:
O how they will
    sway
     swirl
    like dream-seas,
like the richest,
    freshest
      fantasies:
and free,
    free,
as I can never be,
    can never be.

Manila
November, 1979

JOURNEY

The first day away
is always good:
miles and miles out
as in the path of birds,
whose fluent, unerring flight
implies there's some other shore,
some new windfall
which shall surely loom
out of the vast ocean
like a dream, a miracle.

Fool!
You cannot see
that a miracle
will not materialize;
you cannot believe
that there is no home
other than the one you've left behind,
or think you've left behind.

Don't you know yet
that all journeys
are illusory?
That, in fact, you can take
no journey at all, at all,
if your heart is dead,
if your heart is small?

But you're not truly
as naive as you pretend,
wanting only to throw proprieties
to the winds, the winds;
so much so,
foreknowledge
does not deter
your going.

Forever following rumours of
    a new land,
       a new continent,
          a new government,
            a new faith,
            a god.

Seeking all of these,
    and more,
when you're really seeking
    a new you.
But there's really
    no new you.
It's as simple as that,
as simple as death.

Nevertheless,
you want to follow the flowing tide,
subjugate yourself to motion,
although the tide going out
will only come in again;
it will only go out
and come back in again.

June, 1980

60

ANTAEUS

You, who live in the city,
will one day wake up
alone in a white room
and find you have
given away your name.

The sedative night is over,
and you have slept right through
the groans of the drunk in the gutter,
the moans of the young whore
abused by coarse fingers.

So the first light fall
brings no felicity:
there's no one to touch,
save yourself, who have
become unknown to yourself.

Where have you come from?
Where are you going?
The whitening sky has no reply:
only the prospect of day
hardening into mountain.

You poise on the rim of time,
hunger gnawing at your heart,
but for what, you do not know;
only that your hold is tenuous, as you
listen to the locomotive of commerce

Once so familiar,
grind into your very bones.
Now the city sounds become abstract,
turn eerie and strange,
clarified by the black air.

There are no songs from the birds,
only the pneumatic drills

61

digging into the earth,
only the pounding of the piles
deep into your guts.

And the cars rush past,
impatient, snarling like lunatics,
while the ambulance, wailing its tocsin,
carries the green woman with her belly cut open,
leaving crimson tracks on your brain.

Yes, sights and sounds to commemorate your city,
the capital of the colony
of idiots and dummies
who weld your bones to the steel scaffoldings,
feed your sweat to the mad machines.

Now all your blood is gone,
and your life made small,
swamped by the trash
in vogue in our time, the avalanche
of words without meaning.

So one morning you will lie in bed
and realize the enormous lie
you lead; you have let time
slip through your fingers like sand,
while wild stallions stampeded down the strand.

It becomes increasingly difficult,
not that it had ever been easy,
to find a wholesome equilibrium,
to find a way out, instead of making
statements of intent like small, small winds.

It is then you must think of Antaeus,
whose strength came
from contact with earth,

and fill yourself with a
homesickness for the real world.

The time has come for you to walk free,
you, who are sons and daughters of the earth,
brothers and sisters of the sky and seas,
kindred of stones and trees
and companions of the stars in space.

Remember the ancient, true songs
sung in celebration,
remember the peasants, fisherfolk, simple men,
remember the timeless words of the poets,
the ever fresh voice of the wind.

To soothe the soul,
you must go
see birds in flight,
leaves shivering under the stars,
the rainbow arching up the sky.

The hills will provide
redemption; the seas,
renewal; the clouds
tousling across the sun
will be your playmates.

Then it is with grace
you come back to life,
cleansed by the blue air,
and return, like Antaeus,
innocent at last to earth.

THE GIRL FROM ERMITA

If you ever come to Manila,
come down to red-light Ermita
Where nightly I ply my trade.

They call me Fely,
I was born in Samar,
I'm the girl with the bird in her head.

Yes, a bird in my head!
If you look deep into my eyes
you can see it flying about.

You ask what kind of bird it is?
Why, a white gull of course!
For I was born in Samar by the sea.

And how did it get there;
this white gull in my head?
Well, it flew in when I was fourteen.

But you don't really want
to hear the same old hard-luck story!
There are no new legends anymore.

Better take me away somewhere,
take me in your sweaty arms,
and your eyes, cold as death,

Can feed on the peach of my skin,
your savage heart
release its black secrets.

You can do what
you like with me,
I know all the positions.

Come, lie with me
and I will be your love.
Don't you believe me?

Yes, come lie down with me,
it will only cost a hundred *pesos*,
and it's good therapy.

I'll give good value for your money,
I have the techniques
learned through ten thousand nights.

I will embrace you
and the stars outside
will mind their own bloody business.

The wind will not complain,
the trees not grumble,
and all the cops have been bribed.

Or perhaps you think yourself too grand,
too good and holy
to pay to lie with me?

Perhaps you're afraid
the universe will roar in disgust
if you pay for my body?

Don't you know by now
life's a market-place where
you can buy cow meat, goat meat and my meat?

I was born in Samar in Visayas
where the sea ran silver when I was a child
and clouds and trees were my friends.

Of my own father,
I only know
he was a *carabao* of a man.

And like the *carabao*,
he was patient and ignorant,
his feet stubborn in the loam.

But his eyes.
I remember his eyes:
they held such innocence!

When I was twelve, he died,
and my mother and I
lived on, any old how.

Come to think of it,
I don't know how we did it!
Then my mother remarried.

We shifted to an old lean-to
with my step-father.
I had turned fourteen.

For a time I was content enough.
I was only a child then and you know
how children can grow smiles even out of a dungheap!

Then one night my step-father
laid his hands on my green breasts,
and I was too petrified to move.

66   I endured for many months
my step-father's hands
till one night I could not suppress my cry.

My mother came to intervene:
it drove my step-father wild
as a mad, rampaging bull.

He punched me in the face,
kicked my mother in the ribs,
left us black and blue.

The next day I drew
a real deep breath
and ran away from home.

The ferry boat crossing the sea
delivered me from my past:
my childhood lay like broken glass.

An hour after
we reached Cebu city,
I got myself picked up

By a dirty old man
who fed me, gave me shelter and clothes,
and treated me like a household pet.

I was surprised how soon
I got used to his caresses,
no longer reacting with nausea and tears.

So five years passed.
Five Christmases and five Easters
I stayed with my dirty old man.

In our second year
I bore him a bastard girl:
a child, when I was myself a child

Of sixteen.
But already the months
began to wall me in.

When I was eighteen
I went with a handsome man
who took me away to Batangas.

For a brief few months
I blossomed like the *sampaguita*
with this first young man in my life.

A tangerine time it was,
with ice-cream on Sundays,
dances and kisses under the moon.

And then it was over.
His wife came screaming for our blood
and he returned to her like a pup.

Well, life's like that.
I came to Manila
in search of fame and gold,

But found only dust
in the crowded streets
of the capital.

I became a salesgirl
and had to sleep with my boss.
I became a go-go dancer,

Ground my bum in the faces of fools
who drooled like rotten fruit,
while klieg lights tore at my skin.

Now I'm landed here
where life has got me in its jaws
and I no longer wait for miracles.

I no longer care
to look into the eyes of my johns,
for they hold no more secrets.

Now I simply lie flat on my back,
my face upturned to the sugary sky
which the stars eat like white ants.

Now I fuck for a refrigerator,
or for my daughter's school fees:
my girl's just turned eight this May.

Yes, I will turn a trick for a meal,
and men can take me
in any position they wish.

The white scream never flies
out of my black mouth,
the radios will remain silent,

The newspapers advertise soap,
the priests launder
the limp souls of their sinners.

Yes, at night I can be your sweet mango,
but come the dawn,
I'll be as sour as a *calamansi*.

There's still some acid in me,
you know that?
You, who sit there listening so dumbly!

So I've unloaded my story
and my head's just an empty hole
with nameless echoes in it.

Are you quite sure
you don't want
to take me to bed?

Come, lie down with me,
I will be your true love,
for only a hundred *pesos*.

But you only laugh
green and gold and purple
and fly free into the night.

For you are the white gull
who left secret spaces again
inside my head!

But if you ever come back to Manila,
come down to red-light Ermita,
where nightly I ply my trade.

They call me Fely,
I was born in Samar by the sea,
I'm the girl with a hole in her head.

Batangas–Manila
November, 1979

AT ANAWHATA
for Jan Kemp

Here I am,
fallen on bad times,
the sky broken
over my own fair city,
and am driven,
at least for a while,
to this ancient land
whose true hierarchies
are the sun and the sea and the wind:
not the temporal powers
of politicians.
But can the elements
and all the myths of antiquity
expiate my pain,
or teach truth and wisdom
to a profane and ageing poet
who makes so much
out of his own unbelieving?

Anyway, here I am,
feeding the fire
in the old iron stove
inside a little hut
lent to me
by Michael Neill;
it was once
a railyard signal box
at a former station
named Swanson:
wherever that was
            or is;
which some mad nut
  brought all the way
            out here
            to perch
  400 or so odd feet
    above the water

<pre>
              at Anawhata!
                  Whata
                perfectly
                    crazy
             thing to do!
</pre>

And I must
be crazy too,
(though not
   perfectly),
sitting in here
when I should be out
where the winter wind
might forage through my mind,
explore my face,
every line and crack of it:
to test this stranger,
probe his source.

O Western Wind,
Hauauru,
I wish
you could
lay your fingers
upon me,
define me
for me!

Or pluck and toss me out
high over the sea,
over the smooth brow
of Tangaroa,
the Ocean God,
so that I might be cleansed.

Dear Michael,
this is truly
such a lovely room,

such a lovely little station
        to cross
on my short journey
to find the gods.

Not only Hauauru
and old Tangaroa,
but so many others
I can feel
lurking about
here in Anawhata,
here amongst the Waitakere Ranges.

And not only gods,
but ghosts
from those far gone days
before the *pakeha* came.

I have felt them already,
the *mana* of those ancient Maoris,
during the drive out here
through the deep reserve,
the *nikau* palms,
the *toitois* marking every curve
as the small track
wound deeper and deeper,
and farther and farther
away from the city.

From the range,
I saw some lonely knolls
by the sea,
some outcrop of rock

where a time-lost *pa*
might once have been sited.

I was expecting
not this little hut
but some *tuaahu*,
some sacred place for divination;
or to see a tattooed warrior
laying down his *mere*,
letting his woman
welcome me
with a *karanga* call
to the *marae*.

And now, dear friend,
I grow sad,
brooding on battles lost
by those brave warriors
to the musketry
of the *pakeha*:
your forefathers,
Michael Neill!

Forefathers
fathers
us

So many battles
lost

So many won
won and lost

I wonder
for those who won
what was their gain?

I can see only
cities and cities
squatting now
where spring green valleys

had once lay
fabulous in the sun
and in the rain;
where *kiwis* used to strut
in the rich darkness,
careless that men
call them half-blind.

While man
is often purblind,
especially about himself.

Out here,
I can hear
old Tangaroa
announce his domain;
tonight, he sounds
quite benevolent.
But Hauauru,
how he howls
against this wayfarer:
O so proud, primordial,
blasting his *haka* all the way
across the Tasman Sea.

At my feet,
the flax
bows its stiff leaves,
protesting
in a shower of sound
like that of flickering rain.

From another hill,
a lone cow
moos unseen
in the cold night,
mourning for what
I do not know.

Only
I sense
the stars,
only fear the stars
might drop
into the sea.

At this remove,
on this very height
where sea and land and sky
conjoin,
I suddenly think
of my home,
my voyage
from my wife and kids,
and of why I'm here.

What is it I seek?
Another way of life?
Is there really
another way to live?

Is there a way to die?

Is there any choice?

And if there is:

Then, to live:
I want to live like now!
And to die:
I want only when the time comes.

And when my time comes,
it will be westward
to be engulfed by the sea,
like Hinerangi over the glittering
pathway of Tane

to the realm of
Hine-nui-te-po,
benign protectress
of *Rarohenga*,
the assembly place of souls,
where old Ra, the Sun God,
presides golden over a cloudless sky:
just as this late afternoon,
the way he set, spilling gold
over Anawhata.

Or I could go,
perfectly willing,
kneeling to bestow
a last kiss
upon this earth,
before giving back
this body
of little worth,
performing
the ceremony of *tangi hanga*
to help send
my spirit on its way.

Then my insides
will explode
to fatten the grass,
fatten the trees,
and then the trees
with their fat berries
will fatten the wood pigeons,
until, finally,
my bones, cleansed,
will be free
to thunder
their chant
to time.

*   *   *

And now, after sleep,
to find
yet another morning,
is a miraculous event,
as the light dances in
while the tiny room
is still wood-smokey.
Outside, through the wide windows,
I see the hills stand
against the light,
clad with soft green clouds,
daubed by the *manuka* scrub
and the taller *ti* trees,
and the surface of the sea
diamonded,
winking shafts of sun
back at me.

Warming these same bones,
once so cold,
tired with the hours,
into hot lava stone.

And I run out,
for there is
so much to know,
climb up a cliff-face,
clinging onto tough grass tufts,
crops of conglomerate
volcanic rock
up and up and up
like an intrepid goat
biting the substantial air.

I look down upon
a lush valley
breath-taking
from the top,

and especially
that one
particular tree
extending
its dead-white branches,
stripped of their bark,
reaching
like skeletal smoke
caught sculpted
to the sky,
while its roots
eagle claw
the earth,
digging deep in,
not letting go.

And I too,
at the summit,
will not let go,
will not, will not!

    O Tangaroa
   I hear your roar
     Ha-ru-ru
     Ha-ru-ru
     Ha-ru-ru
    O Tangaroa
     I too
   want to roar
     Ha-ru-ru
     Ha-ru-ru
     Ha-ru-ru
    O Tangaroa
   I want to live
     Ae Ae Ae
     Ae Ae Ae
     Ae Ae Ae

AROHA
AROHANUI
AOTEAROA

Anawhata, N.Z.
June, 1980

TAHITI : 20.6.80

All night as the plane
worked to windward,
I am again dispossessed
of family and friends,
ideas and wisdom,
  every dream,
  every notion
  of fantasy;
the mind unquiet,
remaining word-awake,
unable to jettison
the thoughts
  as the hours sit
like an uninvited guest
  on my lap.

Night has turned to black stone,
  rebuffing thoughts
which drift like clouds,
words which drift like birds,
and both magic and meaning
will not form around
the thoughts, the words,
bury them like warm earth
or water or love.

O Tahiti! Tahiti!
I'm coming
to chase a dream
embedded in the
bluest realm
  of my ocean,
strung unreachable
  so long
like gems across my days
and the longest nights.

Unlike my antecedents
who came in search
of a new world to conquer,
new sources
of wealth to plunder,
I'm drawn by the legend
of a noble race
       leading
an idyllic existence:
a happy, carefree people
who know how to laugh
and dance and sing,
and most of all,
who know
       how to love.

I've come to find
a way of love
       to construct,
not so much my past
       but my future,
which seems
so ineluctable.

And so I arrived
with hope and with prayer
as dawn was breaking
over the island.

      *   *   *

"It's not as good
as it was before,"
said my friend Steve,
who'd known Polynesia
twenty years or more.

Earlier, I had appeared
at his schooner,
The Third Sea,
pale as a ghost
from lack of sleep
and too much booze
the night before
and the night before.

The waterfront at Boulevard Pomare
pulsated with noise;
there was as much hustle in the air
as any town, anywhere.
So Science and Technology
and the neon claws of Progress
have reached these distant shores,
have intruded into all our marrows.

O Tangaroa!
Is this all I can find
after this long journey,
find the very thing
from which I fled?
Impossible land
beyond the oceans,
where are all your gods?

And just as I thought
I had lost them all,
a Tahitian crossed the street
to greet us;
he came bare-footed,
dressed very simply,
but I sensed
his head was filled
with good thoughts,
his eyes
with museum greens.

FORTUNÉ AND
LEONIE TESSIER

And so I met you,
as though ordained by the gods,
Fortuné Tessier,
whose fortune is happiness,
great *toere* player,
avid student,
ardent teacher,
advocator of Polynesia
for the Polynesians.
I knew at once
here was a man
wise in his ways,
and I knew then
that Tahiti
was not irretrievably lost.

From you I learned
of Taaroa, the great god
who created everything,
and learned
that Nature is mother,
is bountiful
and will provide
well enough for man;
her bowels rich with minerals,
her lands lush with vegetation,
her seas prolific with shells and fish.

So there is no need
for meaningless work,
no need to work for profit,
but gather Nature's largesse
with your hands,
plough and sow and plant,
or head out in a canoe
to spear fish,
while the children

climb up the mango tree
to shake down the ripened fruit.

But man, alas,
misuses this wealth,
this legacy for all;
he digs deep into her bowels
for uranium and plutonium
to manufacture nuclear bombs,
which they blast
      nearby
at Mururoa Atoll.

      O Paranoia!
The disease which afflicts
great nations
and powerful men!

O Fortuné, who have become
taio, my great friend,
taae, my brother,
how we lamented
over man's fallen state,
growing heavy with sadness,
talking deep into the night,
      about man
who is not free,
but has become entrapped
by material things
everywhere, everywhere.

I shall remember the day
you showed me the hills at Punaauia;
your home filled
with old stones and *tikis*,
which you knew and respected.
Upstream, in the afternoon,
deep into the green,

we picked wild coffee beans,
touched the precious, hardwood *tou*,
drank the wild water.

When we came down,
you showed me the broken *marae*,
its *tikis* and stones
man-used, ancient,
looted to fill
the museums of France;
you also taught me
how to munch
the central leaf stalk
of the *ti* tree,
which is good
for the voice,
you said.

I shall remember
the long nights of music
and the great feasts
of *poisson cru*
onboard *The Third Sea*
with Harold Stephens,
with Dave and Judy Loomis,
when you and Leonie
sang as though you had
ten thousand songs
drawn from all the islands.

Leonie,
who saw through me
straight away,
comforted:
"We all
must make mistakes;
then we know
what is good;

remember sea water
and sun
always purify."
And Leonie,
whose fortune is love,
promised to lay her hands on me,
for she possessed the powers
of her ancestors,
of their spirits,
so that I might be healed;
and you both promised
that before my departure,
you would name me,
in the Tahitian tradition.

In the company of such good friends,
simple under the heavens,
I lay contented, languorous,
always with Tangaroa
pumping through my blood,
while you and Leonie
talked wisely,
spun tales
of Tahiti, of Tuamotus
and the other islands,
talking way into the night
as though the night,
and life, were too short.
And you were right!
The nights only lasted
till the candles sputtered and died.

Sometimes I would fall
into a half-sleep
under the seance of words
        and, at last,
listen to the earth
which had fallen silent;

        and once I heard
        some deep voice call,
ordering me to fly
to high Orahena
whose heights were clothed
in mist and mystery,
where the great primordial twins,
godly bird-men, perch
in all their finery of feathers.
O if I could fly out there,
I would return,
sweep over the world,
and shower blissful
sleep over men!
But, alas,
my wings are pared,
for I am not pure.

        I know now,
when I leave Tahiti,
that I must learn to love.
There is, in the glances
passed between the two of you,
such a numinous, open
dalliance of lovers,
you are indeed suspended
        in a love
that is without rules,
        and full
of intimate joy;
and it makes me
long and long for Margaret,
        my sweet wife.

                              Tahiti
                              June, 1980

BERNARD MOITESSIER

Old sailor,
when you talked to us
as dusk gathered
silently over the sea
and Papeete trembled
on the edge of night,
I wondered

Who can tell
where and when
the journey truly begins,
and also
where and when
it truly ends?

I thought that
perhaps you might know,
    who have solo-
circumnavigated the world,
that you might have
a clear answer,
having been put to the test.

I expected that
you, ancient mariner,
who have crossed such frontiers
of fear and of despair,
must have returned
    free,
filled with a wealth
of knowledge and wisdom
earned ten months out
alone at sea.

The seas must have whispered
such secrets in your ear,
the winds must have sung

a thousand litanies
unknown to man,
the firmament illustrated paths
as you steered by the stars.

But when you talked,
O sailor,
havened in this port,
of how you now
want to promulgate
two hundred characters
of the Chinese script
to unify mankind;
of your plan to plant fruit trees
all along the streets of France;
of your disenchanted attempt
to recreate another world
out here amongst the simple men;
you talk as though
you can lift ignorance
from men's eyes
simply by writing letters
to the Chairman of
the People's Republic of China,
or to fifty French mayors
throughout the provinces;
        and worse,
beguiled by your own
mastery of the seas,
you think you have the power
to bring a new order
to men who have more
than enough of orders.

I knew then
that you did not
know it all
and I felt,

once again,
the taste of time.

    I guess
one can circumnavigate the world
and only come back to the beginning,
which can be mistaken for the end.
    I guess
one can be mesmerized by distances,
measure out a journey in miles,
but achievements such as these
are of no importance.

Yes, perhaps
it's imperceivable
how a journey begins
and how it closes.

Perhaps we are
forever doomed to journey,
unfurl the sails and go,
like the firmament itself
(but O how casually!)
revolves without cessation.

So man must seek
and forever fail;
we may seek
but something always
remains hidden;
that is the rule:
it is shown
in the silence
of the stars.

Is there
a realm of love
without rules?

Did you find love,
old sailor,
in solitude,
isolated by
a thousand leagues of sea
from other men?
The sea which is loving
and merciless.
In the desolation,
did you find
quiet joy?

Perhaps
when the dolphins gambolled
beside your boat,
or when you encountered
the sperm whale
doing just what it was
ordained to do?

And you could not understand,
and did not need to understand,
but in the hush,
                    hear
a presentiment of music
    as time   pushed
impassioned through your bones?

But I have been harsh,
old sailor,
We must all take our chances,
we're only permitted
to return to land a while,
a reprieve beyond which
we'd flounder
like fish on concrete.

May you rest well,
old sailor,
adjust your soul,
and may the clear sky
spread a blue mantle
over your weary bones,
for after the agony,
another journey begins.

And when yours
begin again,
may you return
to first things.

And may we grasp,
you and I,
that that is what we live by.
For we must know that
in our continuance

We are exiled.

Tahiti
June, 1980

SONG OF *THE THIRD SEA*

Life begins for us around sunset
when we gather on the deck
and watch it fall behind Moorea

When we do nothing more serious
than talk and sing
and drink wine in the mild June weather

Yes, I'd rather be on a schooner
with my good friend Steve
than in a hundred other places

That I know of; to lie in the bowsprit net
like a gilded fish
beguiled by the orchestration of the sea

While skipper Steve fusses over his boat,
gentle, laughing, with jungles
and lost cities tangled in his eyes

and crew Dave and Judy Loomis
of Williamstown, Massachusetts,
love the boat to spic and span

Dave singing his songs of sailing
in the Galapagos and the Java seas,
rocking to the rhythm of the waves

> *Hoe Ana E*
> *Hoe Hoe Hoe*
> *Hoe Ana E*

Urge the sturdy rowers
in their long canoes
skimming by the starboard side

Hoe Ana E
Hoe Hoe Hoe
Hoe Ana E

Beyond the breakers
they cross the channel to Moorea
as stars break over the water

Hoe Ana E
Hoe Hoe Hoe
Hoe Ana E

O let us mortals defy our fate,
encourage the great drums,
the *toeres* throbbing the air

The Fete is almost here,
so bring on the wine
and bring on the wine

I want to be like the bronzed
pagan men in the long canoes,
be free to run with the *mahi-mahi*

Spend my years remaining
away from the din of cities,
the world's affairs

So why set my heart on strife?
Come bring on the wine
and bring on the wine!

Tahiti–Penang
December, 1980   *95*

AT THE SALOON BAR IN PAPEETE
WITH HAROLD STEPHENS

Inveigled by Marama,
the round moon
fattened on wine,
we escape each night
from the enigma
of the modern man,
    slip beyond
the clutch of governments,
lose all our cares
down at the Saloon Bar.

Two aging seraphs
crusading for mirth,
coasting along the waterfront
like a pair of tipsy gulls,
or wild gypsies
having a last fling,
in that tough joint down
by the backwaters of Papeete.

The red room spawns
a forest of smiles
and we know nothing
can go wrong there,
where people gather
to live out the night
with the aid of Hinano beer,
and the great gift
of mortal laughter:
to have a good time,
be true to oneself,
take each other as we are.

There one night we found
your old friend, Suzie No Pants,
whom you have written about
when she was once queen

of the famous old Quinn's Bar,
now running to fat,
washing dishes at some restaurant
to support her five kids;
but she showed no signs of regret,
living on her memories
        of a hundred lovers
in the days when the ships came in,
in the days gone by.

Here we've seen old nocturnal women
        regain their youth,
fat matrons with pink cotton dresses
        and rotten teeth,
when they dance and sway, spontaneous,
to the urging of the guitars and ukuleles,
become once again their lissom selves,
svelte, oval-eyed, or their similitudes,
        which they knew
they had never truly lost,
activating their hips
in a wild *tamare*,
they can still enthrall the hard men
with whiskers on their lips
and flowers in their hair.

Yes, at the Saloon Bar
it seems impossible dreams
can be unmoored by the storm
        of Hinano beer,
by the strumming of the gay guitars,
and one can almost believe
        in love's constancy:
that old love never dies,
        if we don't let it!

Tahiti-Penang
October, 1980

BIRD WITH ONE WING

The black winds of evening
rustle along the quayside,
tonguing the bones of the houses,
lapping the lees of the hills
until whole hills are lost
       to the darkness,
and we can claim at last
some kinship with the stars,

Who scrawl their age-old script
a million light-years away,
ignored by a faithless world:
the power of man increases
with the decline of the times;
under the lamp-light,
dust from a hundred nuclear
fallouts shower the air.

For we relish only fire;
      our souls,
not knowing what to believe, continue to hunger,
planning factories and governments
to reach into our bones:
everywhere the gendarmes patrol us,
armed with walkie-talkies and truncheon sticks.

Now darkness is upon the world,
and all things are possible;
other echoes inhabit the present,
borne upon the waters of the past,
those silver-filled seas of antiquity;
we become involved with shadows,
congruent with nameless dreams,
with the moment's pure movement.

Sense and place dissolve,
present, past and future
run into new shapes

        like driven clouds
in squalls across the mind:
we can no longer grasp
verities, nor know
the lie of the land.

And possessions do not suffice,
nor the company of friends,
nor yesterday's love:
they are as a floating cloud
and will become nothing
undone by the faint moonlight,
the reek of magnolia and wine,
drunk with the world's revolving.

I am the bird with one wing,
never knowing when to return
        from the night
shaped with malevolence,
catching the paranoia of the times
        when tribes and nations
contend for their vaults
filled with skeletons.

The human heart hoards many stones,
        spurns the due seasons,
the simple truths
        within our grasp;
our heads over-stuffed
        with useless knowledge
only empirically derived,
enervated by the wrong riches.

What can comfort these old bones?
Shall I plunge into the unknown,
        abandon thought,
        the burden of money,
the choice of staying aloof from life,

and be like Gaugin at Punaauia,
    prosperous stockbroker
turned penurious painter?

Far better to go dancing after
the damsels with the gazelle eyes,
frolic with *vahines* on the beach,
    be light of heart.
If I can return to my own people,
do nothing more serious than sing,
perhaps I may live up to my new name,
    Te Manu Tini.

The fleeting world is but a stream,
so let the heart shed its care;
    blood and sinews untied
will ride over the rocks in gay cascades;
let us surrender youth and grief
to time, that sacred river;
the passing years will slip away
and flesh returns to ashes and to earth.

                    Tahiti
              June, 1980

HOMECOMING

But now

Margaret, my *tiere*,
my sweetest flower,
without you,
there is nowhere to go.
Without you,
even so brief a journey
has been too long.

Now

When the red sun drops
from an ailing sky
over these unfortunate isles,
and the lagoons, once blue,
turn a transparent white,
the fragrance
of hill flowers
suffuses the evening.

Here

I, newly named
Te Manu Tini
with the power of a thousand wings,
want to mount the sky,
combat every storm
and the deepening distance
to return to your arms.

But your

absent eyes
have stolen all my strength,
stranded here alone
when all other birds have migrated home,
and my deep passion

for you burns rivers within,
while the thunderous surf outside,
pounding against the reef,
tears my heart into shreds.

You know

I love every earth I see,
though some say
I carry with me a prophetic sadness,
wanderer on a cloud,
wounded by governments,
intoxicated by tinsels
spewing out of factories,
disturbed by the gendarmes
who police the streets:
and most of all,
a dim-witted fool
who strayed away
from your love.

The fate

of a bird with one wing
is, one would imagine,
not to fly at all
but tethered to the ground,
to dream eternally
of becoming the wind,
which, driven by whims,
can occupy the skies:
but why do I wander
when all my world is you?

An abandoned,

hollow shell on the beach
perhaps can best echo the words

of those who have lost everything,
those who have lost
love and freedom,
garnering the songs
of each stray soul
and resounding them
to the empty heavens.

Alone

one night in Moorea,
watching the moon
whitening the lagoon,
my heart was bursting with songs
and you were not there to listen:
so much so I was stricken
with a mute anguish.
O *ti* tree,
whose inner green stem I've tasted,
grant me now voice
to sing of my beloved,
my wife, my lodestar.

Later

that same night,
my head disjointed
from a bad mixture
of wine and beer,
my intestines scorched
by the stale booze,
I lay sleepless and then
had a *moa-moa-a*,
a Tahitian name for a dream
in which one can see
into the future.

It was

a dream about you:
when, upon my return,
you came towards me
with that faraway look
in your eyes,
as if it was you
who had been wandering,
and in that hurt look,
I sensed a real fear
of losing you.

How

you must have suffered
living with this vagrant poet
forever flailing at the stars,
when it's governments
I should contend against,
who make victims
of all men.

Enough

for the moment;
remove the instrument
from the path of the wind.
Don't listen to howls
and prayers and speeches,
but filled with time and space,
sing the love song
of my homecoming.

Long hours

are falling like withered flowers
scattered on the moist hills;

the black winds
are blowing me out of time
and it is due season
to return home.

My heart

newly fashioned by distance,
labouring past
these days and nights
has learned at last to open,
so as to give,
and to receive love,
where, my love,
my journey ends.

Moorea
June, 1980

EPILOGUE AT CAMPUAN, BALI
for my eldest son, Kasan

What more can I ask
for my forty-fourth birthday
than to be here in Campuan
with all
my loved ones near?

I have travelled far
over the years
in the world amongst men,
of money and of power,
and did not once suspect
that paradise on earth
is so easy to find.

I was right to trust
the fairy winds
straight from the moon
which brought me here,
heed the magic words
from a time
before the word was bought.

In the first light
I rose and saw
Gunung Agung
a thousand rice-fields away,
silhouetted in the flowing red,
but miraculously impermanent:
as if ready to be spirited
away by the gods!

And as the long night
was gradually being swept away
by the fantastic brooms,
the far fields were lit,
and then the near,

to reveal the ancient terraces
worked by a silent
succession of men.

But the padi are still a young green
and the flowing stream
at the foot of the hill
washes all impurities away;
O how my blood responds
to this land of temples and rice,
of clouds and sun
and sky which hold
all worthwhile knowledge!

The world's affairs
are more than miles away
here amongst the farmers
whose work will never be done,
but is done willingly;
and who do not want to see
beyond the next crop's yield,
        the latest betrothal,
        the newest birth,
        the coming festival
        at the local village:
knowing that the prospects
        for the next year
        and the next
are never known.

The clouds and sun and sky
have more understanding,
while man can only accept it whole
        if he is blessed,
        if he is endowed
        by an act of faith:
and that is the only secret
worth knowing.

My heart and head
are both quiet again
in this natural world
where all around are rich rice-fields,
and all around are men at work
with their sickles and *cangkuls*,
not knowing nor caring
how close I am to them:
and I know once again
that Asia is my home,
here where I am sure
of my way.

OM SWASTIASTU!

Bali
July, 1980

SPRING MOON BLUES

SPRING MOON BLUES

How to live now, my dear,
with the moon so full
on this warm Spring night?

You know how it is
when hours are disposable,
traded away for surface, for safety,
something misleading,
which, in the end,
proves unworthwhile,
reached without risks,
without true striving,
when always, always the mountain
can only be climbed by daring,
only by daring.
Have we really forgotten?

So how to live now, my dear,
with the moon so full
on this warm Spring night?

Vancouver
April, 1987

WITH MARGARET AT
JOGYAKARTA

On our second honeymoon
in twenty years or so,
we took an evening ride by *bechak*
through the bumpy, old streets of Jogya
to catch a fragment
of the Ramayana dance
at Dalem Pujokusuman;
the air moon-cooled,
the dust settled at last
after a hard, hot day
brings a freshness to our years
which I pray, my sweet,
will wear as well
for yet another twenty.

Java
1982

BALI REVISITED – 1983

Every so often I come here again
as though in quest of a cure,
taking a personal risk
speculating for a grand trance.

Composing words in exorcism
not so much to set down thoughts,
map out abstract meanings,
as to expunge them.

Every so often I've enough
of the city,
of unmasterable modern life
where speeches, advertisements, other
minutiae, pile high into mountains.

Though my hair is turning white,
turning white, I know nothing important,
only some set responses
suitable for the social occasion.

I'm afraid of becoming a robot,
programmed, practical, efficient,
would rather be stone
left carelessly out among the elements.

Even though I know by now
nothing's exempt from wear and tear,
erosion by the salty air,
the consequence of never-ending rain

And of words, words, words.

Tandjung Sari, Bali
1983

A WINTER VACATION

Jet-lagged from a flight
half-way across the world,
at last we unwound with a stroll
along the shores of Lake Zurich,
spending our family vacation together.

The steepled, old cityscape
dusted with recent snow,
the jagged Swiss Alps,
magical chunks of vanilla
across the stretch of cold, grey water
were new nuances,
unreal, dream-like
in the soft morning light.

We wandered through whiteness,
a purity one would imagine
commensurate with awed silence,
yet, at first sight,
my younger kids, quickly inspired,
clearly yelped with seraphic joy,
proclaiming their intuitive license
to frolic in the snowy fields,
gathering loving armfuls,
to savour like favourite fairy tales.

"Do you know every single
 snow flake is different?"
exclaimed Kajin, my third-born, eleven,
with a child's wise, unspecialized knowledge,
a mind as yet uncontaminated
by life's tutored pragmatism.

Kakim, my youngest, the most inquisitive,
has not yet learnt to care, bless him,
as he pays no due consideration
to anything except an astonishment

at all the wonders and random
treasuries around him.

Kagan, my second son, at fourteen,
is already more restrained,
defining himself, beginning
to discover the bewilderment,
the contradiction between man's world
and that of cosmic nature.
O why must age makes us so grave?

Our eldest son, Kasan,
whom we sorely miss,
is back in Singapore
performing his National Service,
thrust into the serious
business of soldiering,
truly steeped into the
tragi-comedy of life.

While my wife and I,
full-flowering adults,
keep ruminating over and over
the same old anxieties:
how to salvage coherence,
find peace of mind in our time,
which always seems so elusive.

All the while, my words
like fresh snow,
after falling from all that height,
turn ephemeral, soon melt
on hard, implacable ground.

Zurich
1983

SUMMER AT REPULSE BAY

The moon diminishing
to a lovely vestige,
a slim scimitar,
preens herself
in the sky clear
above the shimmering bay.

A Saturday night crowd
of happy youngsters
gather to share
the simplest joys:
pleasure in companionship,
passionate kisses,
their gleeful yelps, laughter
winging upwards

To dance with the moon.

Hong Kong
1984

DUBLIN REVISITED – 1985

for my second son, Kagan

Thirty-two years separate
my first coming here
and this brief visit with Kagan;
the big gap in between
populated by so many ghosts,
figments of personal fiction
which I try to catch, repossess,
but it's difficult, elusive
when they play, tease like leaves
touched by summer sunlight,
shaking in the breeze.

I sniff the same air
eager for scents from the past:
the aroma of a good coffee brew
at Bewley's on Grafton Street,
drunken breath of worn-out men,
smell of the shawled, slum women,
and then there were the easy, rouged girls,
when with wild poet friends
we frequented favoured pubs –
Davy Byrne's, Jamet's, Mcdaid's –
dreaming young of the good times
and how it felt
to be totally free.

There was no such thing, of course,
even in those green days,
though now it gets harder every year.
Enough of this misting of the eyes
like an old goat
afflicted with selective memory.
Enjoy this happy moment
at the Abbey Tavern at Howth
where Yeats once used to stay,
supping with companions, Roddy Carr, Patty,
some new-found friends,
relishing my first pint of well-pulled Guinness,

which, doubtless, is good for me,
though it's no potion nor panacea
for all the ills that fill one's life.
We are all ignorant of the past,
doubtful about our future
and can only sigh, as Tu Fu did,
for the clumsiness of his life's course.
Some things stay the same.
The grey clouds outside
make the Irish evening sky
look thoughtful, like a man
brooding over dark events,
and I'm reminded again
that nobody's life is perfect.

It's sensible to keep the secrecies of the past,
quit this manoeuvring at night
around furniture in the unlighted house,
for the past can hold treacheries,
those proverbial skeletons in the cupboard
best left as they are:
blurred, unclear shapes,
be they gems or garbage,
in the subsurface
of the shifting, changing sea:
and get on with this business of living.

I see Kagan by my side, at fifteen,
enrolled this year at Bryanston
as I was at Blackrock so long ago;
lonely, apprehensive,
first time away from home;
yet eager, excited,
a young student in a foreign land
ready to set out
on his own big journey.
I can only love him and say,
my son, do not be afraid.

County Wicklow, Eire
1985

INSOMNIAC

Wish my mind a white patch of snow
a bird would leave imprints freshly on landing
in place of the thoughts, the thoughts

Vancouver
1986

HORNBY ISLAND

*for Billy Little, who shared loved spots
and fond friends*

Here on the headland by Downe's Point
we cast dreams to rise
synchronous with eagles and gulls,
all make-believe, egocentric,
near to fanatical,
else aim true to roam deep
with Leviathan in the ocean's mind,
free from perplexities and profundities
such as bind the scheduled self.

Here is the arbutus grove
whose trunks and branches tighten
like nerves, twisted witnesses,
victims of shapely winds
which blow in always unseen,
sweet from the south
or coming cold from the north,
                    from every direction
the prevailing force of nature.

Wish I could emulate the arbutus,
slough off my thin skin as easily
as these native trees their bark
from abrasion, disdain or design,
unveiling the bare beauty
of strong, hard wood beneath.

Over on Fossil Bay
the rot of herring roe
strewn amongst broken clam shells, dead crabs,
on dirty grey sand, exposed bedrock,
thickened the morning air,
but gave no cause for bereavement:
these millions of botched birthings!

And none also for the Salish,
no open lamentation for a race
almost obliterated without trace
from their native habitat,
save a few totems, some evidences of middens,
a score of petroglyphs of their guardian spirits
carved a thousand years ago
on smooth flat rock by the shore,
of killer whales, Leviathans again,
to guide their hunts,
the destiny of their tribe.
Having retraced them
gently with finger tips,
they now guide mine.

Vancouver
April, 1987

GATE OF HEAVENLY PEACE

We woke early that Sunday in the cabin,
watching the summer morning
wash up upon the lake shore,
the surrounding firs and junipers
on the sides of sprawling hills
flamed green in the fresh light,
the water calm, smooth as oil.

Suddenly, a flock of birds took flight,
scattering like pieces of white paper
blown across the clearing
filling the air with raucous cries.

Then our sons told us
about the massacre at Tian An Men.
They'd heard the news over the radio
around 3 am, Newfoundland time.
Ivy, our hostess, and wife of Calvin Payne,
had the radio on all night by her bedside,
either because she couldn't sleep
and needed distraction,
else wanted some reassuring tie
to the outside world,
here, in this secluded retreat
by the lake beyond Portland Creek.

"Some bad, bye!"
Calvin said, shaking his head.
"Two thousand people killed,
three times the population of Cowhead!"
That's the outport on the west coast
where Ivy and Calvin lived,
and where I was working as the local doctor.

"Shooting their own children!"
Ivy exclaimed, as she busied herself
preparing the traditional Jig's dinner
of salted beef and potato cake,

boiled turnips, carrots and cabbage;
Calvin switched the radio to a favourite station
for their staple diet of Sunday morning country music;
we sat on the sunlit deck
listening to plangent songs
about unrequited love and broken hearts.
It was hard to focus on the fact
that they were mowed down
in the hundreds that day in China:
young men and women
chests and backs shot full of holes.

The night before, when the sky hatched stars,
Calvin and I sat out sipping Johnny Walker,
unlocking words in the darkness,
failing to sight the Northern Lights;
Calvin recounting the hard life
in these parts when he was a child,
before Confederation, Welfare, UIC,
before the much-loathed Resettlement,
before the road struck north.
And I was thinking,
after spending more than a year amongst these folk,
how hard life still is in this province,
with its underdevelopment, chronic high unemployment,
with the recent big cut in the cod quota,
the closure of fish plants on the coast.
The future's bleak for the children
who either depart to feed
factories and mines in Ontario,
else stay and eke out a living
jigging cod, snaring rabbit,
working the short lobster season,
repeating the harsh cycle of life
led by their fathers and forefathers.

My friend Calvin's an exception.
He has laboured hard since boyhood

and now owns Payne's Sales and Service,
operating a diesel and gasoline pump,
a Ford pick-up agency,
a Yamaha skidoo dealership,
the tender for snow plowing the roads in town;
in addition, he drives the school bus,
and only recently, won the concession
to clean up the Shallow Bay Provincial Park
on the outskirts of Cowhead.
Whew! He makes me breathless.

Ivy herself has charge of
the family grocery store
with occasional help
from her daughter-in-law, Kay.
Ivy, who was born and raised in rural Labrador,
says she's considered an outsider
in spite of having settled in Cowhead
for twenty years,
another reality about outports in Newfoundland.
As a doctor, I have often chided Calvin
for working too hard,
but he laughs and brushes me aside:
"I loves it, bye!
I'm fit and strong."
Perhaps he's haunted
by privations of his past.
Still and all, he retreats often
to this small cabin in the wilderness,
which he built with his boys some years before,
hauling in materials by skidoo and sled
in winter, the most accessible season;
rest of the year, the terrain's boggy and wet,
almost impassable.
Here, he can renew himself,
cast for sweet lake trout,
bag his moose for the year.

124

It's simply a good place to laze about,
a haven from the mad turmoil of the world.

Yet, from this same lake
just three weeks earlier,
they'd pull out the House girl
barely twelve years old,
too late for resuscitation
by the time they summoned me.
I remember her body
lying on the back of the battered Ford pick-up
vivid in a flowery costume,
her hair straggly and wet,
lips blue, cheeks like porcelain,
pupils fixed and dilated
like the eyes of the cod fish I've seen
flopped upon the decks of dories
when they come in with the catch
on late summer evenings
by the small town jetty.

At the House's home that afternoon
in Daniel's Harbour, an adjoining outport,
I saw the father, Big Max,
seated by the oilcloth-covered kitchen table,
beating his head hard with his large fists
and wailing for his darling girl:
"I can't live through this, mother.
Don't ask me to live through this!"
I attended to the old grandmother
who'd passed out in her rocking chair
by the small front parlour,
rallied around by family and friends.
I kept hearing Max's implacable cry:
"I can't live through this, mother.
Don't ask me to live through this!"
All the while wondering why
he's addressing his crushed, weeping wife, Rosie,

rather than fate, or the gods.
Poor Big Max, he was wrong of course.
He can live through this.

And so can we,
this infamous Sunday of June 4, 1989,
relaxing on this near-pristine lake,
watching the air dancing above the water,
the golden light spreading like butter
on the green hills,
and not doing anything about
the red blood staining the Square
they named Tian An Men,
Gate of Heavenly Peace.

Cowhead, Newfoundland
1989

WINTER NIGHT

In a night

when the wind veered many times,
a lone stranger
uncertain of its way,

when the winter rain, though never fervent,
was bent on shrinking the soul
with its incessant commentary,

when old memories returned to haunt,
each one made accountable,

I sat and listened to the wind and the rain.

Vancouver
1986

AUTUMN IN HALIFAX

Leaves gone so quickly from the trees
Almost from one week to another,
Stripped away by an unseen wind.

Words locked so mutely in the mind
Perhaps are forever lost and,
Unlike the leaves, unrenewable.

Brown ducks and grey gulls sit
On placid water by Point Pleasant Park,
Oblivious to the November chill,

Passing of the years, family, friends.

Halifax
November, 1989

A N D   T I M E

The way the clouds
chase
after memories
this afternoon
as if to devour them,
makes indelible designs
on the mind,
reappraising
correspondence of self
and time.

Vancouver
1995

FATHER

So the sky
did not die with you.

Still brandishing its blue
after these past four years
and may persist,
at least
for the next forty,
beyond which
I shall surely not last
    myself –
turning away from the light
like your final
pain-torn days,
so terribly far away
from me.

To cross over into what?
    What's
on the other side?
That, I shall never fathom.

To me,
your life,
with its vicissitudes and crises,
is like a river
flashing white
in the depths of night,
unknowable,
unshareable –
each of us
on our own
lonely journey
guilty about the gulf between us
that we could not completely mend,
just as we're all
to be forever blamed,
since named at birth.

Yet, all through our daily
and our nightly
        lives,
there was a kindling love,
an illuminating love –
yes, there was,
surely, there was.

INUK SHUK

As dispensation for enduring
dull routine for a week,
I was permitted to leave
the chronic psychiatric ward
in St. Paul's Hospital
for a walk, unwatched, unescorted
towards nearby English Bay.

It was just as well!
I was going crazy
pacing and repacing the same steps
along familiar corridors,
going nowhere,
simply killing time
when time was hard to kill;
sometimes, I swear,
it almost stood still.

On admission, I'd surrendered
my shaving kit
as well as my initiative,
obeying all instructions
like a good kid.
I was brought in
for electro-convulsive therapy
to treat Major Depression
and Parkinson's Disease.

Growing old, that's what it is,
a natural course,
the body caught
in the process of degeneration,
too many days now
falling between the cracks,
just run of the mill, ordinary
days that make up much of life,

come and go without surprise,
without consecration.

Now all's nearly done,
there's no turning back
trekking the back streets
of the heart,
so to what purpose
have I prepared myself
to wait for what might never come?
And if it should never come,
would I still feel betrayed?

Where are the dreams
which once proliferated
wild like scented jasmine
upon the tropic plains
from whence I came?

I recall one time
of dull, grey skies,
river swollen at year's end,
all the fields flooded,
I had a sudden urge
to walk away
from the sameness of my days.

What am I doing here
while the day is racing away
and I have not lived?
Stop playing games with time,
must stop.
Sit still,
keep eyes closed,
think of nothing.

O faraway faces all gone
under the earth, disintegrated,

                        and life –
was it wholly imagined,
those familiar acres
now grass-grown,
beyond the sweep of years,
green purlieus
eluding my grasp,
and for which I feel
a longing, a nostalgia,
if that is possible,
for what I've never possessed,
never known,
only festering and festering
in my heart?

O father, I've been cheated,
cheated!
But of what?
I've tried to live with it,
with a faith bordering insanity!
Never simple,
just never.
When I only seek
still pools of the day,
dream spaces,
simplicities.

I must be strong.
The sea laughing,
uncomplicated.
Watch it laugh.

Sky's a bright mirror
in my head,
idiosyncratic, apocalyptic
as quick, quick
sickness takes –
an unrelieved whiteness

spreading across the terrain
with no visible supplements
to thwart the take-over.

Then came upon
grey granite stones
piled on the beach
high against the sky,
resembling a human form
with arms outstretched in welcome
as I tumbled into its embrace.

It was an Inuk Shuk,
ancient symbol of Inuit culture
traditionally a landmark
or navigational aid,
well-known figure
of hospitality and friendship
in the far, northern wastes.

It had seemed, at first,
so irreconcilable to the here
and now of Vancouver city,
yet this mass of stones
assembled by human hands,
manages to reach out to me
with a healing spirit
across time and distance,
giving succour as I take
this walk alone
on a bitter, wintry afternoon.

Vancouver
December, 1996   *135*

WAKE FOR CHARLES WATTS

Summer's beginning
    to end.
Beethoven's Fifth
on CBC Radio Two
pours out of the kitchen
onto the back deck
where I've been idling
    washing me down
onto our small back garden
which Margaret, the boys and I
started creating some four years back,
when we tried to make the house a home.
Actually, the garden
was more Margaret's passion
    than the rest of us.

Come to think of it,
it was about the same time
you told me you had cancer
when we met strolling down
    Commercial Drive,
the main thoroughfare
    in our neighbourhood.

Now, leaves are already yellowing,
wilted flowers waiting to be
    dead-headed,
plants and trees
    cut back
for the Fall,
for Winter
the small ceremonies
of living
and dying.

And this, one of the last
    golden afternoons
when the other world

seems far away
        or
perhaps very close by.

Vancouver
August, 1998

THE OLD GATHERER OF
STARS DANCING THE SALSA
AT MAMA MIA'S

Well, they say there's no fool
    quite like an old fool –
Who knows, perhaps they're right.
But whatever the appellation,
it's really not so bad
    being a fool,
going after a good time
on a night wild with stars.

    On such a night
I would want to stumble out
    into the darkness,
grab hold of some stars,
gather an armful of them to my breast.

    Yes! To love life.
Be unrepentant, incorrigible.
    For I know
one night there will be nothing left out there,
    nothing,
or else I will simply not be there
    to catch the stars
        anymore.

So let's drape some glad rags
upon our paltry frames,
    go strut our stuff
    down at Mama Mia's.
Tap our feet to the gay music,
    salsa the night away
with the beautiful women
    who enjoy flirting,
        imagining
we're falling in love again with love
    even if it's unrequited,

and make a laughing spectacle
    of ourselves.

    Afterwards,
spill out onto the fresh wintry night.
    silly smiles spread
    across our faces,
follow the cobble-stoned streets
winding through the old walled city,
    And join old Li Po
    fellow gatherer of stars
when he went to rescue the pale moon
in danger of drowning in the river,
    that night
O so many centuries ago.

San Miguel de Allende, Mexico
1998

OUR BACK GARDEN, VICTORIA DRIVE

So brief, really
are these weeks of summer
conjured out of our back garden,
that I should not hold on to them,
    simply let go.

    There,
    one sigh
    and they're gone
      forever.

Vancouver
June, 1995

GLOSSARY

Ae Ae   (Maori) agree; yes

Antaeus   in Greek mythology, the god of Libya, who
   derived his strength from contact with the earth.
   According to legend, he compelled 21 strangers to his
   country to wrestle with him and every time he touched
   the earth, his strength was renewed.

Aotearos   (Maori) Land of Long White Cloud, the Maori
   name for New Zealand

Aroha   (Maori) affection, love

Arohanui   (Maori) great love

bechak   Indonesian pedicab

bersilat   Malay martial arts

Blackrock   Irish public school in Dublin

bomoh   traditional Malay healer

Bryanston   English public school in Dorset

calamansi   (Tagalog) a green lime

cangkul   (Indonesian) a hoe

godown   warehouse

Gunung Agung   holy mountain in Bali

Ha-ru-ru   (Maori) roar

haka   (Maori) song accompanying war dance

Hinerangi   the beautiful daughter of a Piha chief who
   married a young chief from Karekare. They were exceed-
   ingly happy until one day while fishing, a huge wave

engulfed the group he was with and Hinerangi's husband
was carried out to sea and drowned. Hinerangi could not
be consoled. On the headland hight above the restless
ocean, she sat for days endlessly searching the seas for
signs of her husband until she too, made the final journey
westward over the glittering pathway of Tane to be with
her husband. Even today from a certain position on the
cliff, one can trace her life-size figure gazing out to sea, a
sculptured form carved by the restless elements of
Tangaroa, the ocean god, and Hauauru, the west wind.

Hoe Ana E, Hoe Hoe Hoe   a chant used by Tahitian canoe
rowers

Jig's dinner   a favourite Newfoundland dish

kampung   small village

karanga   (Maori) welcoming hail

kiwi   (Maori) wingless nocturnal bird

Li Ch'ing Chao   Chinese woman poet 1084-1142

Li Po   Chinese poet 701-762

mahi-mahi   (Tahitian) dolphin

mana   (Maori) influence; prestige

mandore   foreman

Manu   (Tahitian) bird

manuka   (Maori) tea tree

marae   (Maori) enclosed ground used as a meeting place

Marama   (Tahitian) moon

mere   (Maori) short flat weapon made of stone or green-
stone

moa-moa-a   (Tahitian) nightmare

Moitessier, Bernard   French sailor who has circumnavi-
gated the world and written extensively of his exploits.

nikau   (Maori) a palm

Om Swastiastu   Balinese prayer invoking peace to
mankind

Orahena   the highest mountain in Tahiti. According to leg-
end, it was inhabited by twin brothers who had wings
and could fly like birds.

pa   (Maori) a fortified village

pakeha   (Maori) white man

poisson cru   (French) a dish of raw fish marinated in lime
and coconut milk

Rarohenga   (Maori) the underworld

rokok economi   cheap cigarette

rokok istimewa   expensive cigarette

sampaguita   (Tagalog) jasmine

sampan   small wooden rowboat

taae   (Tahitian) brother

taio   (Tahitian) friend

tamare   Tahitian dance

Tane   Tane to the Maori represents many natural phenom-
ena including light, which he is said to have brought into
the world. The Maori believed that when a person died in
the Waitakere Ranges, his spirit travelled to its final
abode over the glittering pathway of Tane, that ribbon of
light formed by the rays of Ra, the sun god, across the
billowy realm of Tangaroa, the ocean god.

tangi hanga   (Maori) Maori funeral ceremony

ti   (Maori) cabbage tree

tiere   (Tahitian) flower

tiki   (Tahitian) sacred stone

Tini   (Tahitian) thousand

toere   (Tahitian) Tahitian drum

toitoi   (Maori) a tall feathered grass

tou   (Tahitian) a hardwood tree

towkay   boss

Tu Fu   Chinese poet 713-770

tuaahu   (Maori) sacred placed used for divination

vahines   (Tahitian) women

ACKNOWLEDGEMENTS . . .

are due for poems previously published in book form –
Eyewitness by Heinemann Educational Books (Asia)
Ltd., *Lines from Batu Ferringhi* and *Bird with One
Wing* by Island Press, Singapore. Apart from omissions, some revisions have been made for this selection.

I also owe thanks to the publishers and editors of a
long list of anthologies and magazines in which poems
for this selection first appeared.

For the encouragement and help with this selection, I
wish to thank Marisa Alps, Jim Wong-Chu, John Pass,
Gerry Gilbert, Billy Little, and not least, my family for
their constant love and support.